DATE DUE

	PRINTED IN U.S.A.

TODO SOBRE EL INVIERNO / ALL ABOUT WINTER

Gente en invierno/ People in Winter

por/by Martha E. H. Rustad

Editora consultora/Consulting Editor: Gail Saunders-Smith, PhD

CAPSTONE PRESS
a capstone imprint

Pebble Plus is published by Capstone Press,
1710 Roe Crest Drive, North Mankato, Minnesota 56003.
www.capstonepub.com

Library of Congress Cataloging-in-Publication Data
Rustad, Martha E. H. (Martha Elizabeth Hillman), 1975–
  Gente en invierno = People in winter / by Martha E. H. Rustad.
    p. cm.—(Pebble plus Todo sobre el invierno/All about winter)
  Includes index.
  Summary: "Simple text and photographs present people in winter—in both English and Spanish"—Provided
by publisher.
  ISBN 978-1-4296-8241-1 (library binding)
  1. Winter—Juvenile literature. I. Title. II. Title: People in winter.
  QB637.8.R87 2012
  508.2—dc23   2011028793

Editorial Credits
Sarah L. Schuette, editor; Strictly Spanish, translation services; Veronica Correia, designer; Eric Manske,
    bilingual book designer; Marcy Morin, photo shoot scheduler; Kathy McColley, production specialist

Photo Credits
Capstone Press/Karon Dubke, all

Note to Parents and Teachers

The Todo sobre el invierno/All about Winter set supports national science standards
related to changes during the seasons. This book describes and illustrates people in
winter in both English and Spanish. The images support early readers in understanding
the text. The repetition of words and phrases helps early readers learn new words.
This book also introduces early readers to subject-specific vocabulary words, which are
defined in the Glossary section. Early readers may need assistance to read some words
and to use the Table of Contents, Glossary, Internet Sites, and Index sections of the book.

Printed in the United States of America in North Mankato, Minnesota.
102011   006405CGS12

Table of Contents

Tabla de contenidos

It's Winter!

Winter is here.

It is cold and snowy.

Winter days are short.

¡Es invierno!

Llegó el invierno.

Hace frío y nieva.

Los días de invierno
son cortos.

4

What We Do

Teresa and Julian wear
coats, hats, and mittens
when they go outside.

Lo que hacemos

Teresa y Julián usan
abrigos, gorros y guantes
cuando van afuera.

6

We play in the snow.
The wet snow makes
good snowballs.

Jugamos en la nieve.
La nieve mojada hace
buenas bolas de nieve.

We play winter sports.
Lilly and Jim go skiing.

Jugamos deportes de invierno.
Lilly y Jim van a esquiar.

Winter Celebrations

We celebrate winter
holidays.
Anna gives her grandma
a gift on Christmas Eve.

Celebraciones de invierno

Celebramos festividades
de invierno. Anna le
da a Abuela un regalo
en Nochebuena.

Carter plays
with a dreidel
during Hanukkah.

_____

Carter juega
con un dreidel
durante Janucá.

Harrison reads
about the seven
days of Kwanzaa.

Harrison lee acerca
de los siete días
de Kwanzaa.

17

Jane's family stays
up until midnight
on New Year's Eve.

La familia de Jane se
queda despierta hasta la
medianoche en la víspera de
Año Nuevo.

Winter Fun

We have fun outside
in winter. What do you
like to do in winter?

Diversión en el invierno

Nos divertimos afuera
en el invierno. ¿Qué te
gusta hacer en el invierno?

Glossary

celebrate—to do something fun on a special occasion or to mark a major event

Christmas—the holiday that celebrates the birth of Jesus Christ

dreidel—a toy with four sides that spins like a top

Hanukkah—a Jewish festival that is celebrated in December

holiday—a festival or time of celebration; people usually take time off work, school, or regular activities during holidays

Kwanzaa—an African-American holiday that is celebrated for seven days in December

Glosario

celebrar—hacer algo divertido en una ocasión especial o para marcar un evento importante

el dreidel—un juguete con cuatro lados que gira como un trompo

la festividad—un día festivo o tiempo sagrado; por lo general, la gente se toma días libres del trabajo, de la escuela o actividades regulares durante las fiestas

Janucá—una festividad judía que se celebra en diciembre

Kwanzaa—una festividad afroamericana que se celebra por siete días en diciembre

Navidad—la festividad que celebra el nacimiento de Jesucristo

Internet Sites

FactHound offers a safe, fun way to find Internet sites related to this book. All of the sites on FactHound have been researched by our staff.

Here's all you do:

Visit *www.facthound.com*

Type in this code: 9781429682411

Super-cool stuff! Check out projects, games and lots more at www.capstonekids.com

Index

Sitios de Internet

FactHound brinda una forma segura y divertida de encontrar sitios de Internet relacionados con este libro. Todos los sitios en FactHound han sido investigados por nuestro personal.

Esto es todo lo que tienes que hacer:

Visita *www.facthound.com*

Ingresa este código: 9781429682411

¡Algo súper divertido! Hay proyectos, juegos y mucho más en www.capstonekids.com

Índice